"This book is dedicated to my wild flower, **Havva Lynne.** Your Dada loves you more than you'll ever know.

Between two mountains,

Next to a forest, all of a sudden,

There, in the middle of the meadow, was a single sprout.

Who was special because she was the first one.

Day after day, this little sprout grew.

Until one sunny morning, she finally bloomed.

This flower was so beautiful, with her colors so bright.

She learned so much that day until her first
night.

The following days were much like the first.

Watching the birds, the bees, clouds, and other things on the earth.

As time went by, she noticed one thing.

"Where are the others that look like me?"

The little flower really wanted another.

A little friend to talk with, a sister or brother.

She sat all alone, learning more in case she could teach them.

Hoping for others to arrive, always searching
for new stems.

One dewy morning, she woke up and looked around.

To her surprise, something new covered the ground.

She was so happy for now, she wouldn't be alone.

Thinking about what to say first and how to tell them all, she knows.

They grew bigger and bigger until she knew the next day they would open.

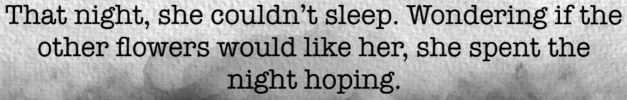

That night, she couldn't sleep. Wondering if the
other flowers would like her, she spent the
night hoping.

What a fantastic sight! A sea of colorful mixture.

"Welcome, I love you!" She said. "You can call me your big sister."

The End

"Consider how the wild flowers grow. They do not labor or spin. Yet I tell you, not even Solomon in all his splendor was dressed like one of these. If that is how God clothes the grass of the field, which is here today, and tomorrow is thrown into the fire, how much more will he clothe you—you of little faith!"

Luke 12:27-28

About the Author

"Warren J. Thomas was born and raised in a small town 45 minutes outside Baltimore, Maryland. In 2008, at 23 years old, due to the tragic passing of his best friend, Warren met Jesus and started to follow his teachings as a Christian. Having moved south to Marietta, Georgia, Warren became a nursing assistant for roughly five years. Warren met the love of his life, Mandy, in 2010, and they married a year later. Shortly after their wedding, Warren felt a calling to open a church that he thought would be in the greater Atlanta area. To their surprise, Warren and Mandy were called overseas to Asia Minor to plant churches. Since 2013 they have successfully helped start multiple churches in their region. Their family of two has also grown to five with the births of their three amazing children. 2018 brought about a new chapter in Warren's life as he started writing a book in his host language. In 2023 Warren began to focus on producing English books for children and adults under his LLC Harvest Harbor Publishing."

68092183R00020